Carolyn Nystrom

Illustrated by Eira Reeves

CANDLE BOOKS

Published in the UK in 2005 by Candle Books
(a publishing imprint of Lion Hudson plc).
Distributed by Marston Book Services Ltd, PO Box 269,
Abingdon, Oxon OX14 4YN

ISBN-13: 978-1-85985-578-4
ISBN-10: 1-85985-578-4

Worldwide co-edition organised and produced by
Lion Hudson plc, Mayfield House, 256 Banbury Road,
Oxford OX2 7DH, England.
Telephone: +44 (0) 1865 302750
Fax: +44 (0) 1865 302757
Email: coed@lionhudson.com
www.lionhudson.com

Printed in China

In the beginning there was nothing.

But there was God.

4

And God made everything
beautiful. God made trees,
flowers, mountains, oceans,
tiny shells, huge dinosaurs,
fluffy clouds – and angels.
God looked at everything
He had made and said,
"It is all good."

Genesis 1;
Psalm 148:1–5

5

The angels lived with God in heaven.
They were His helpers.
But one angel, named Lucifer, said,
"I don't want to do what God says.
I want to be like God myself."

Some of the other angels said
they wanted to follow Lucifer.
God let them, but they could no
longer be His angels.
They had to leave the beautiful
place where God lived.

Isaiah 14:12–15; I Timothy 3:6; 2 Peter 2:4; Jude 6

7

Lucifer's name changed to Satan, or the devil. Ever since, Satan has worked to turn people against God – even me.

8

He began with the first man and woman, Adam and Eve. God told Adam, "You may eat from every tree except one tree. If you eat fruit from that tree, you will die."

1 Peter 5:8–9; Genesis 2

9

Satan went to Eve.
"You won't die," Satan lied.
"That tree will make you wise
so that you will know all that
is good and all that is bad."

Eve wanted to be wise.
"You could be like God," Satan added.
So Eve took fruit from the tree.
She ate it and gave some to Adam.
He ate too.

Genesis 3

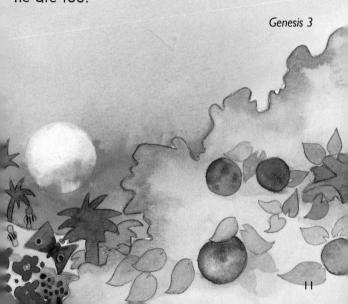

But Adam and Eve did not become like God.
They became sinful like Satan.
They had to leave the beautiful place God
had made for them.
They got tired and sick and hungry.
Finally, just as God had said, they died.

Their children sinned too.
One day Cain got so angry that he killed his brother.
"I don't know where Abel is," he lied.
"I don't have to take care of my brother."

Genesis 4

13

Every person born after that did wrong.
People sinned because they were born
wanting to do wrong.
They sinned because they saw
their parents do wrong.
They sinned because Satan tried
to make them do wrong.
I do wrong things for the same reasons.

Once God sent a huge flood
to cover the earth and its sin.
He saved Noah and his family
in a covered boat.
But after the flood, even that
family began to do wrong.

Psalm 51:5; Ephesians 2:1–3;
Genesis 6 – 9

15

Then Jesus came.
Jesus is different from anyone
else who ever lived.
He never sinned.
Jesus is God's Son.
Three times Satan tried to get
Jesus to do wrong.
But Jesus said, "No."
Then Satan left Jesus alone in
the desert.
God sent good angels from
heaven to take care of His Son.
Jesus is the only person
who never sinned.

Matthew 4:1–11

Because of Adam and Eve,
everyone sins.

GOD FORGIVES

But because of Jesus, anyone can
ask God to forgive.
I can too. And God will.
Then God will treat me as if I had
never done anything wrong.
It's as if God sees only the goodness of Jesus.

Romans 5:12–21

19

God wants me to try
to obey Him.

In the Bible someone asked Jesus,
"What is God's most important rule?"
Jesus answered,
"Love the Lord your God
more than anything else.
Love the people around
you as much as yourself."
That's a hard rule, but it
helps me know when
I'm doing wrong.

Matthew 22:36–40

HOMELESS
PLEASE
HELP

21

Once my teacher was telling a story about Jesus in a storm. I didn't listen. Instead I ran a toy car up and down the table. Then I thought, *Am I loving my car more than I love Jesus?*

Once my mum gave me a banana to
share with my sister.
I gave her a small piece and kept
a big piece for myself.
Then I wondered, *Am I loving myself
more than I love my sister?*

But Jesus will forgive when I ask.
Yesterday, mum asked me to
pick up my toys.
I watched TV instead.

I felt bad when she got home.
Later, I prayed, "God, I'm sorry
I didn't obey mum."
And Jesus forgave me.
JESUS ALWAYS FORGIVES
WHEN WE ASK.
Today I picked up
my toys first thing.

I John 1:9

Satan wants to turn me against God.
He tries by tempting me with small sins
like keeping the big part of the banana
or taking Ethan's ruler because I like it
and I lost mine.

I ask Jesus to keep me from doing wrong.
Jesus lives inside me, and He is much
stronger than Satan.

Romans 7:14; Ephesians 6:10–18; 1 John 4:4

27

I will not always have to fight
against Satan.
In the end, God will throw Satan and
all of his angels into hell.

But I don't have to be afraid of hell.
I belong to Jesus, and God will take
all who are in His family to heaven.

28

We will live with Jesus in heaven forever.

Matthew 25:41; Revelation 20:7–15

Even now God helps me to do right.
Last week my sister left my favourite
book out in the rain.
I wanted to throw all of her books
on the floor and stamp on them.

But I didn't.
God helped me to say no to Satan.
Later Suzie bought me a new book.

I Corinthians 10:13

31

I'm not perfect.
As long as I live, I will do some things wrong.
But slowly Jesus is helping me to live more like He did.
I'm glad.

Ephesians 4:17 – 5:2